Editor
Lorin E. Klistoff, M.A.

Managing Editor
Karen Goldfluss, M.S. Ed.

Editor-in-Chief
Sharon Coan, M.S. Ed.

Cover Artist
Barb Lorseyedi

Illustrator
Howard Chaney

Art Coordinator
Kevin Barnes

Art Director
CJae Froshay

Imaging
Rosa C. See

Product Manager
Phil Garcia

Publisher
Mary D. Smith, M.S. Ed.

Map Skills

GRAD

D1362041

Author
Mary Rosenberg

Teacher Created Resources

Teacher Created Resources, Inc.
6421 Industry Way
Westminster, CA 92683
www.teachercreated.com
ISBN: 978-0-7439-3727-6
©2003 Teacher Created Resources, Inc.
Reprinted, 2011
Made in U.S.A.

Table of Contents

Introduction

The old adage "practice makes perfect" can really hold true for your child and his or her education. The more your child has practice with and exposure to concepts being taught in school, the more success he or she is likely to find. For many parents, knowing how to help your child can be frustrating because the resources may not be readily available. As a parent it is also difficult to know where to focus your efforts so that the extra practice your child receives at home supports what he or she is learning in school.

This book has been designed to help parents and teachers reinforce basic skills with children. The focus is a review of map skills for students in grade 2. While it would be impossible to include all map concepts taught in grade 2 in this book, the following basic objectives are reinforced through practice exercises (refer to the Table of Contents for specific objectives of each practice page):

- identifying symbols
- reading a legend
- identifying road signs
- identifying north, south, east, and west
- measuring distance in inches or centimeters
- identifying locations
- finding coordinates
- identifying continents and oceans

There are 36 practice pages. (*Note:* Have children show all work when computation is necessary to solve a problem. For multiple choice responses on practice pages, children can fill in the letter choice or circle the answer.) Following the practice pages are six practice tests. These provide children with multiple-choice tests to help prepare them for standardized tests administered in schools. As your child completes each test, he or she can fill in the correct bubbles on the optional answer sheet provided on page 46. To correct the test pages and the practice pages in this book, use the answer key provided on pages 47 and 48.

How to Make the Most of This Book

Here are some useful ideas for optimizing the practice pages in this book:

- Set aside a specific place in your home to work on the practice pages. Keep it neat and tidy with materials on hand.
- Set up a certain time of day to work on the practice pages. This will establish consistency. Look for times in your day or week that are less hectic and more conducive to practicing skills.
- Keep all practice sessions with your child positive and constructive. If the mood becomes tense or you and your child are frustrated, set the book aside and look for another time to practice with your child.
- Help with instructions if necessary. If your child is having difficulty understanding what to do or how to get started, work through the first problem together.
- Review the work your child has done. This serves as reinforcement and provides further practice.
- Allow your child to use whatever writing instruments he or she prefers. For example, colored pencils can add variety and pleasure to drill work.
- Pay attention to the areas in which your child has the most difficulty. Provide extra guidance and exercises in those areas. Allowing children to use drawings and manipulatives, such as coins, tiles, game markers, or flash cards, can help them grasp difficult concepts more easily.
- Look for ways to make real-life applications to the skills being reinforced.

Simple symbols stand for different things on maps. Make a simple symbol for each picture. The first one is done for you.

1. 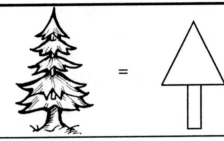 =	2. 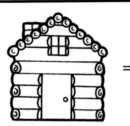 =
3.  =	4.  =
5.  =	6. 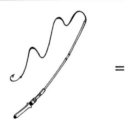 =
7.  =	8. 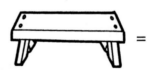 =
9.  =	10.  =
11.  =	12.  =

Coloring a Map

Color the map.

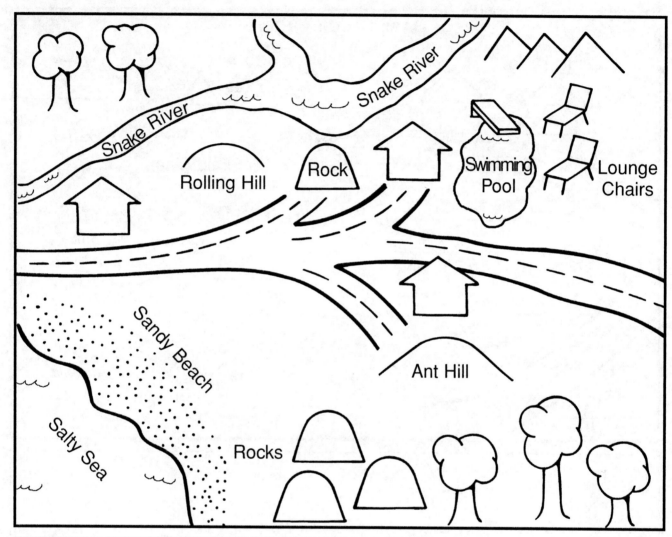

Legend		
= blue	= green	= black
= yellow	= red	= gray
= orange	= brown	= pink

Reading a Legend

Use the map and the legend to answer the questions.

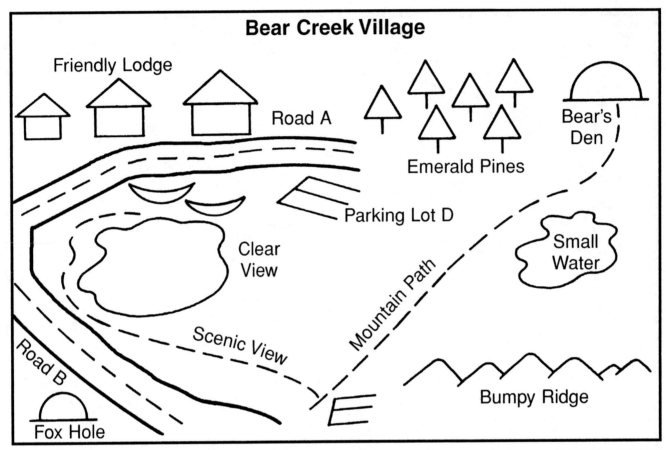

Bear Creek Village

Friendly Lodge

Road A

Emerald Pines

Bear's Den

Parking Lot D

Clear View

Small Water

Mountain Path

Scenic View

Road B

Fox Hole

Bumpy Ridge

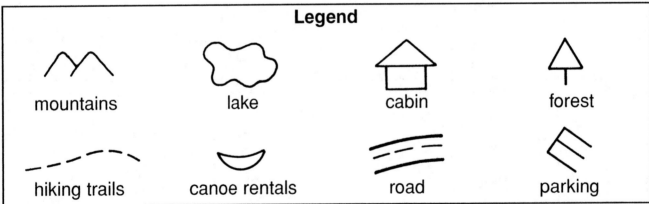

Legend

mountains   lake   cabin   forest

hiking trails   canoe rentals   road   parking

1. How many cabins are in the village? _____

2. What is the name of the forest?_____

3. What hiking trail is the nearest to Small Water? _____

4. Are the canoe rentals closer to Friendly Lodge or the Fox Hole? _____

5. How can you travel from Fox Hole to Emerald Pines? _____

6. How can you travel from Bear's Den to Small Water?_____

A New State: New Liberty

A new state has recently been discovered. Use the map of New Liberty and of its surrounding states to answer the questions.

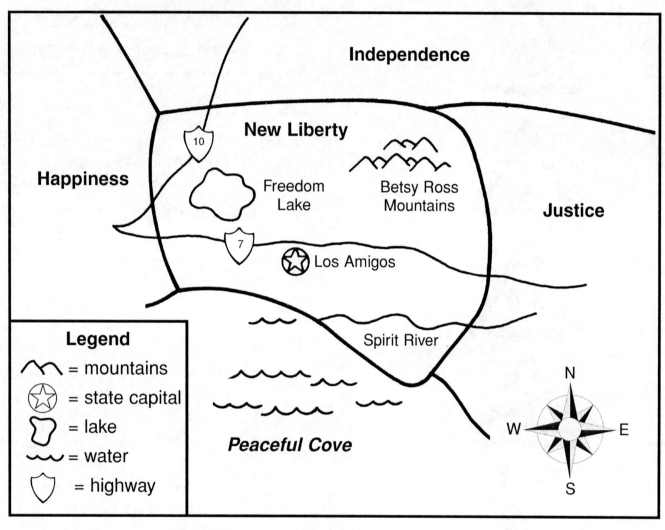

Independence

New Liberty

Betsy Ross Mountains

Happiness

Freedom Lake

Justice

10

7

⭐ Los Amigos

Spirit River

Legend

⌒⌒ = mountains

⭐ = state capital

⬠ = lake

〜 = water

🛡 = highway

Peaceful Cove

N
W   E
S

1. Name the mountain range in New Liberty. _____
2. What is the name of the state capital? _____
3. Is Freedom Lake in the eastern part of New Liberty or the western part of New Liberty? _____
4. Is the Spirit River north or south of Los Amigos? _____
5. Where is Peaceful Cove located? _____
6. Identify the three states that share a border with New Liberty.

   _____, _____, and _____
7. Which highway will take you from Happiness to Los Amigos? _____
8. Which highway will take you from Happiness to Independence? _____
9. Is Freedom Lake east of Happiness or west of Happiness? _____

Road Signs

What does each sign mean? Draw a line matching each sign to its meaning.

1.

> You are driving through a windy area.

2.

> Children are in the area.

3.

> Gas station is up ahead.

4.

> An airport is nearby.

5.

> Train tracks are up ahead.

6.

> You are driving on a winding road.

7.

> Cars are driving in two directions.

The United States

Use the map to answer the questions.

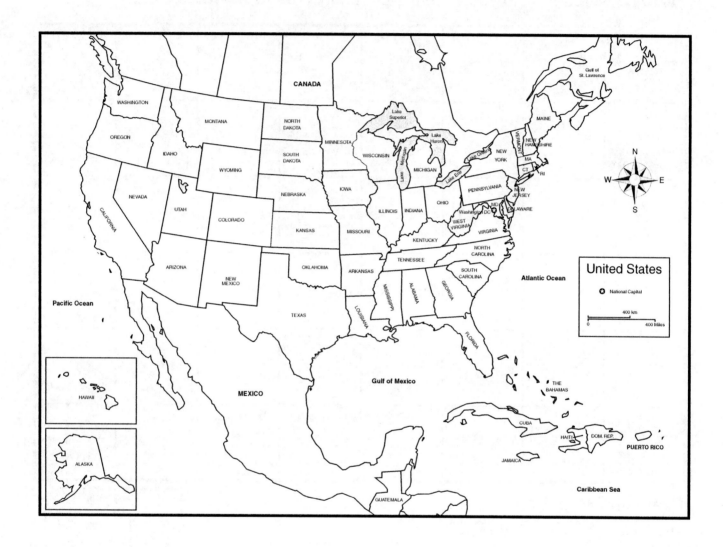

1. I live in _____. Color the state red.

2. The following states border on my state:_____
   _____. Color the states purple.

3. I live closest to the _____ Ocean. Color the ocean blue.

4. The nearest country to the north is _____. Color the country orange.

5. The nearest country to the south is _____. Color the country green.

Vacation Planning

Write the simplest directions to go from one business to the next. Use the following words to help you write the directions: **east**, **north**, **south**, or **west**.

	Backpacking Tours		Passport Photo Shop			
						Ticket Window
		Bus Tours	Luggage Shop			
						Map Store
Cruise Ship					Camera Shop	

Example: Map Store to the Backpacking Tours:
Go <u>west</u> 6 steps. Then go <u>north</u> 4 steps.

Legend

☐ = 1 step

1. Passport Photo Shop to the Bus Tours:_____

2. Camera Shop to the Backpacking Tours:_____

3. Bus Tours to the Map Store: _____

4. Ticket Window to the Cruise Ship: _____

5. Map Store to the Luggage Shop: _____

North, South, East, and West

Use the map to answer each question.

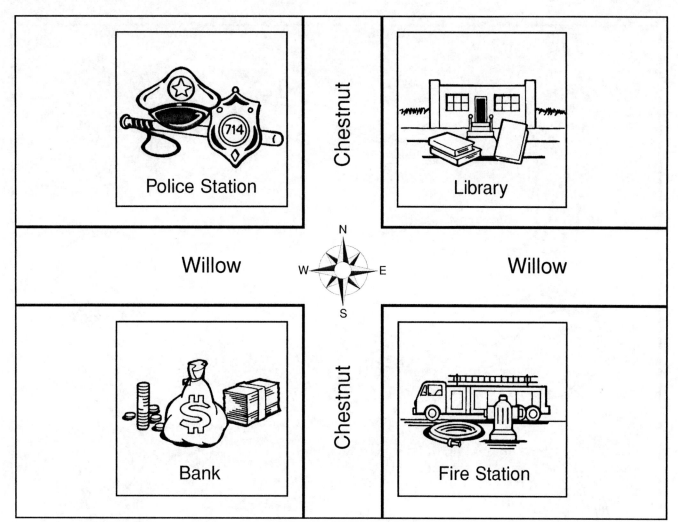

1. Which buildings are north of Willow?_____
2. Which buildings are south of Willow? _____
3. Which buildings are west of Chestnut? _____
4. Which buildings are east of Chestnut? _____

Write the direction each arrow is pointing.

5.

6.

7.

8.

_____   _____   _____   _____

Following Directions

Follow the directions.

1. Color the ball **south** of the girl red.
2. Color the skateboard **east** of the backpack orange.
3. Color the backpack **west** of the boy yellow.
4. Color the ball **south** of the backpack green.
5. Color the skateboard **north** of the pencil blue.
6. Color the backpack **east** of the girl purple.

Giving Directions

Write two different descriptions for each animal's location.

Bulldog	**Turkey**	**Lamb**	**Piggy**	**Bunny**
Kitty	**Bear**	**Froggy**	**Cow**	**Turtle**

Left

←

Right

→

Example: Turkey • Turkey is north of Bear. • Turkey is to the left of Lamb.	**1.** Bulldog _____ _____
2. Cow _____ _____	**3.** Piggy _____ _____
4. Kitty _____ _____	**5.** Turtle _____ _____

Giving More Specific Directions

Identify the corner location of each building using the following words: **northwest**, **northeast**, **southwest**, or **southeast**.

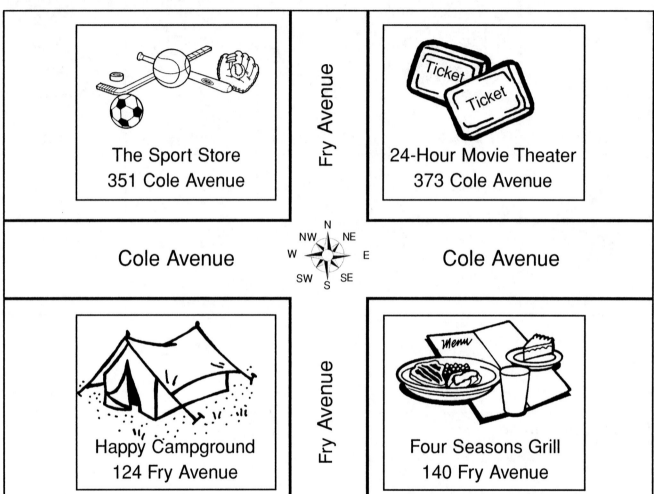

1. The Sports Store is on the _____ corner of Cole Avenue and Fry Avenue.

2. Four Seasons Grill is on the _____ corner of Cole and Fry Avenue.

3. 24-Hour Movie Theater is on the _____ corner of Cole and Fry Avenue.

4. Happy Campground is on the _____ corner of Cole and Fry Avenue.

Writing the Address

When writing an address, make sure to include the house number and the name of the street.

Write each address.

1. Max lives at _____.

2. Orenda lives at _____.

3. Perry lives at _____.

4. Ralph lives at _____.

5. Tina lives at _____.

6. Wendy lives at _____.

Write the Directions

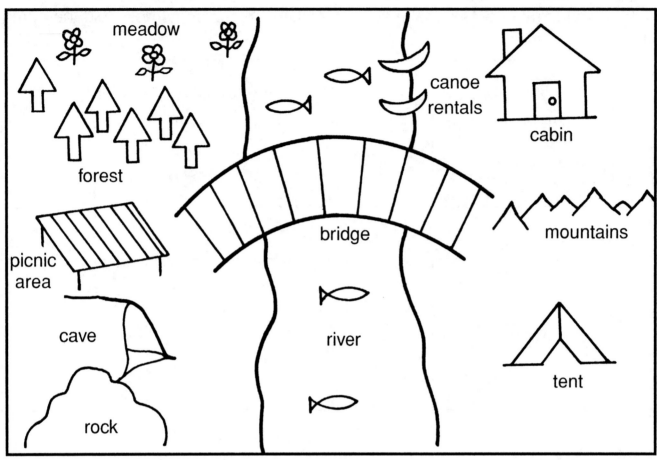

meadow

forest

picnic area

cave

rock

bridge

river

canoe rentals

cabin

mountains

tent

Word Bank

by	east	left	next to	north	over
right	south	straight	under	west	

On a separate sheet of paper, write the directions to each place.

Example: Rock to the tent

- Go north.
- Turn right and go over the bridge.
- Turn right and go south.

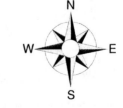

1. Picnic area to the cabin

2. Cave to the canoe rentals

3. Meadow to mountains

4. Forest to the cave

5. Canoe rentals to the meadow

6. Bridge to the rock

Distance in Inches

Answer the questions using an inch ruler to measure the distance between each place.

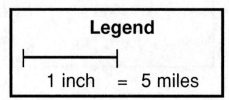

Legend

1 inch = 5 miles

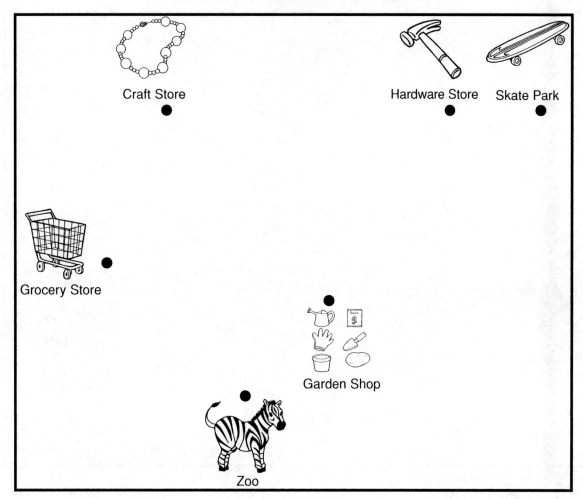

Craft Store

Hardware Store   Skate Park

Grocery Store

Garden Shop

Zoo

1. How many miles between the Zoo and the Grocery Store? _____

2. How many miles between the Hardware Store and the Craft Store? _____

3. How many miles from the Skate Park to the Garden Shop? _____

4. How many miles between the Hardware Store and the Grocery Store? _____

Distance in Centimeters

Measure the distance between each athlete and his or her playing field.

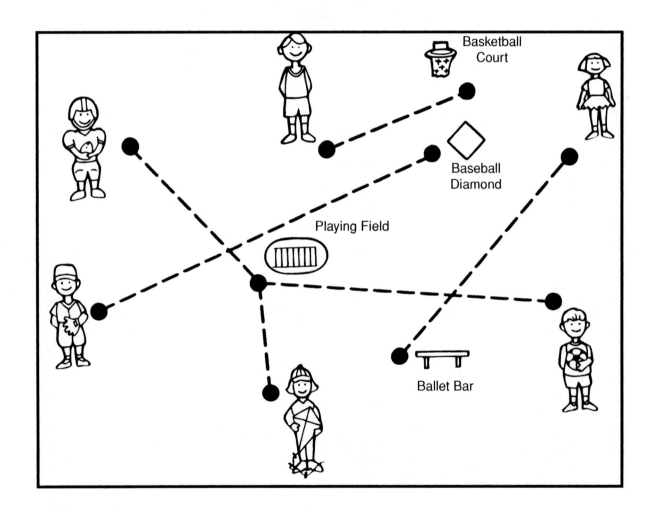

1. Baseball Player to the Baseball Diamond = _____ cm or _____ blocks

2. Ballerina to the Ballet Bar = _____ cm or _____ blocks

3. Soccer Player to Playing Field = _____ cm or _____ blocks

4. Football Player to Playing Field = _____ cm or _____ blocks

5. Basketball Player to Basketball Court = _____ cm or _____ blocks

6. Kite Flyer to Playing Field = _____ cm or _____ blocks

Cross Streets

Cross streets are the nearest major streets to a particular address. One cross street runs north and south. The second cross street runs east and west. Using the map, write the cross streets for each address.

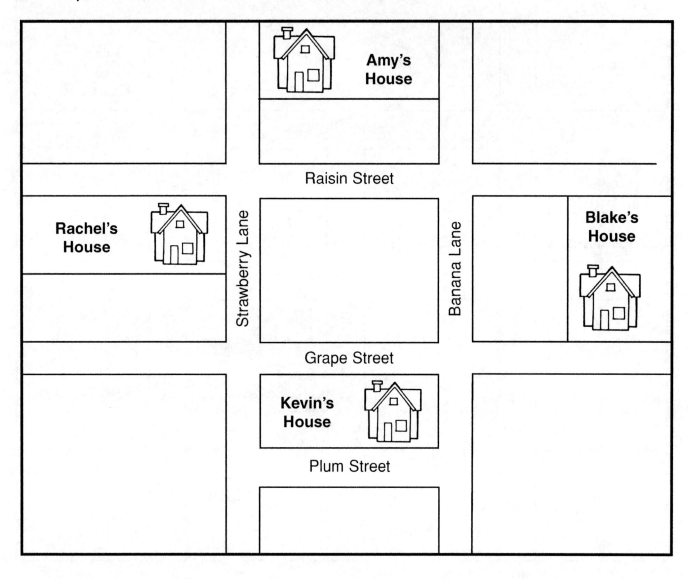

1. The cross streets by Rachel's house are _____ and _____ .

2. The cross streets by Kevin's house are _____ and _____ .

3. The cross streets by Amy's house are _____ and _____ .

4. The cross streets by Blake's house are _____ and _____ .

Parallel Streets

Another way to give directions is to tell the two parallel streets, or streets on either side of a specific address. Use the arrows to help you.

Boats-R-Us

Blue Street

Gifts Galore   Bait Shop

Red Street

Star Avenue   Moon Avenue   School   Sun Avenue   The Cakery

Pink Street

Cars 4 Sale

1. Gifts Galore's address is 221 Red Street. It is between
_____ and _____.

2. Cars 4 Sale's address is 375 Pink Street. It is between
_____ and _____.

3. The school's address is 400 Moon Avenue. It is between
_____ and _____.

4. The Cakery's address is 424 Sun Avenue. It is between
_____ and _____.

Location! Location!

Write the location for each item. The first one is done for you.

	Over →	Up ↑
1.	2	1
2.		
3.		

	Over →	Up ↑
4.		
5.		
6.		

	Over →	Up ↑
7.		
8.		
9.		

How to Get There

Write the directions to go from one place to another. You may only go left, right, up, or down. The first one is done for you.

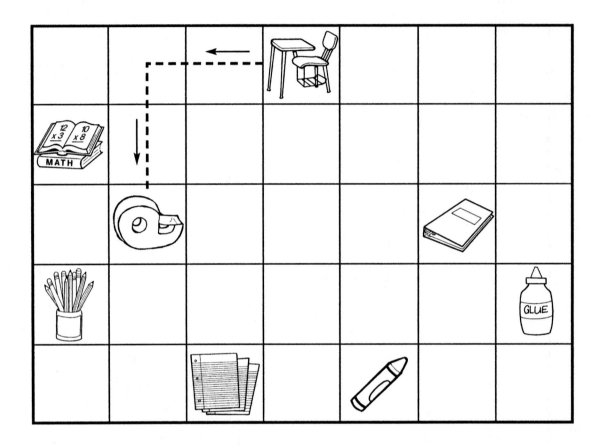

		Right →	Up ↑
		Left ←	Down ↓
1. desk	tape	← 2	↓ 2
2. crayon	papers		
3. notebook	glue		
4. pencils	math book		

		Right →	Up ↑
		Left ←	Down ↓
5. pencils	crayon		
6. glue	tape		
7. math book	notebook		
8. papers	desk		

Using Coordinate Points

Write each animal's coordinate points. Remember to go right first and then up.

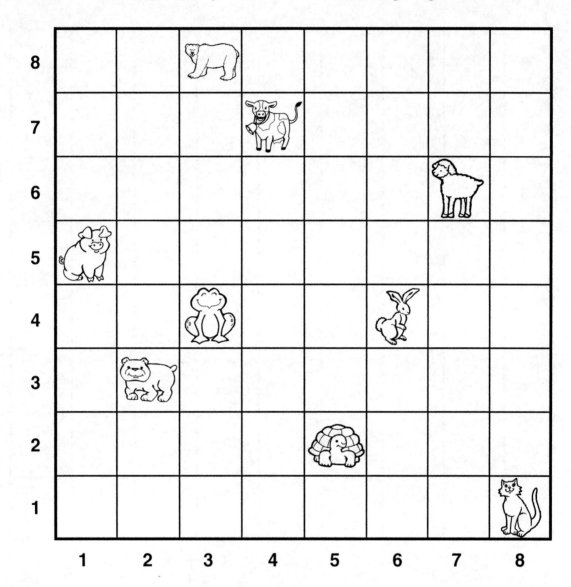

1. (___, ___)

2. (___, ___)

3. (___, ___)

4. (___, ___)

5. (___, ___)

6. (___, ___)

7. (___, ___)

8. (___, ___)

9. (___, ___)

Every Shape in Its Place

Draw each shape in the correct location. Remember to go right first and then up.

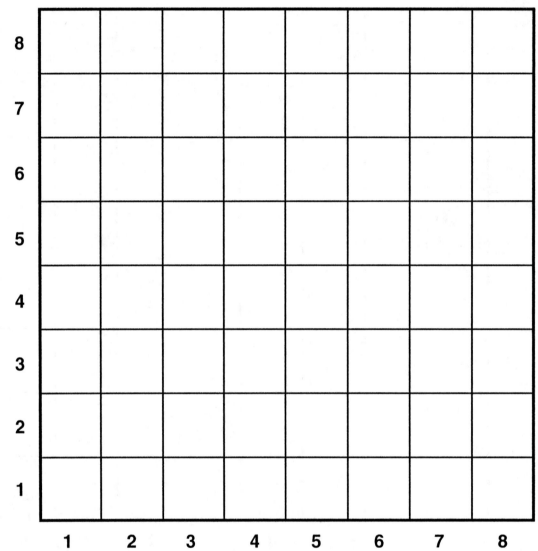

1. (2, 7)

2. (6, 8)

3. (1, 4)

4. (5, 1)

5. (3, 5)

6. (1, 3)

7. (4, 1)

8. (5, 3)

9. (6, 6)

Reading a Map

Write the location of each piece of sports equipment. Mark the letter first and then the number. The first one is done for you.

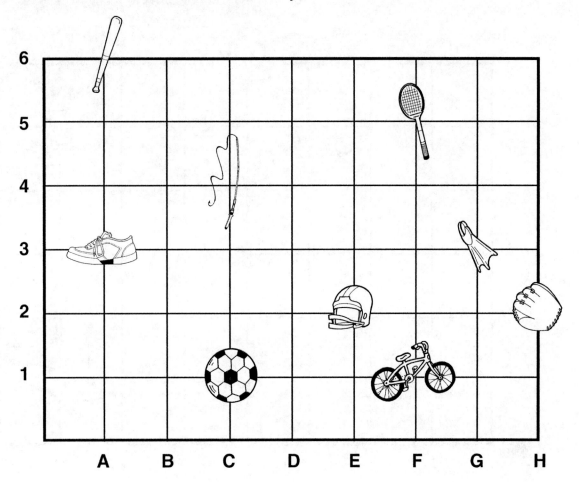

1. bat	(A, 6)	4. bicycle	_____	7. fishing rod	_____
2. soccer ball	_____	5. helmet	_____	8. flipper	_____
3. racket	_____	6. glove	_____	9. shoe	_____

The Golf Course

Write the location of each item found on a golf course. Mark the letter first and then the number. The first one is done for you.

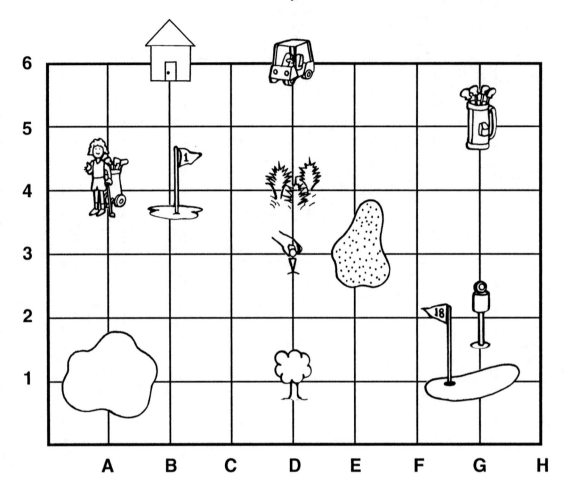

1. (A, 4)

2. _____

3. _____

4. _____

5.  _____

6. _____

7. _____

8. _____

9. _____

10.  _____

11. _____

12. _____

City Streets

Write the name of the item located in the specific part of the map.

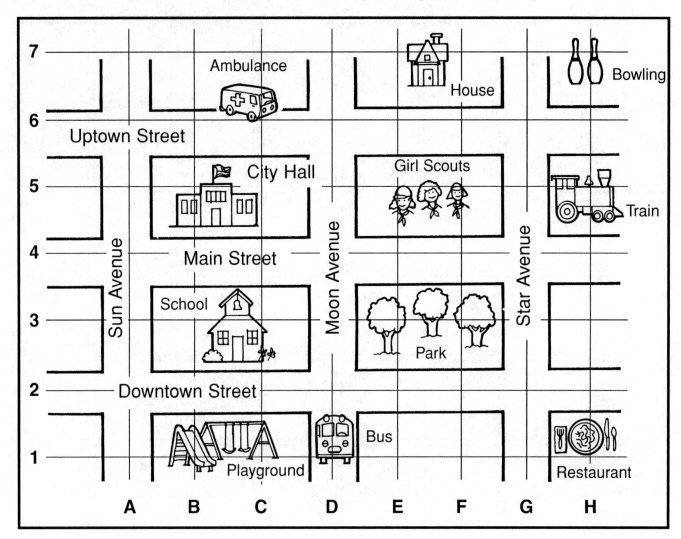

What is located at the following points?

1. (C, 3) _____
3. (H, 7) _____
5. (D, 1) _____

2. (H, 1) _____
4. (F, 5) _____
6. (C, 6) _____

Name the street located at the following points.

7. (B, 6) _____
9. (G, 3) _____
11. (B, 4) _____

8. (B, 2) _____
10. (D, 5) _____
12. (A, 3) _____

All Kinds of Vehicles

Follow the directions to locate the correct vehicle.

A   taxi   race car

B

police car

C   bus

fire engine   train   D

Directions #1
1. Start at A.
2. Go south 3 spaces.
3. Go east 4 spaces.
4. Name the vehicle: _____

Directions #2
1. Start at B.
2. Go north 1 space.
3. Go west 4 spaces.
4. Name the vehicle: _____

Directions #3
1. Start at C.
2. Go south 2 spaces.
3. Go west 2 spaces.
4. Name the vehicle: _____

Directions #4
1. Start at D.
2. Go north 5 spaces.
3. Go east 1 space.
4. Name the vehicle: _____

Reading Road Signs

Use the map to answer the questions.

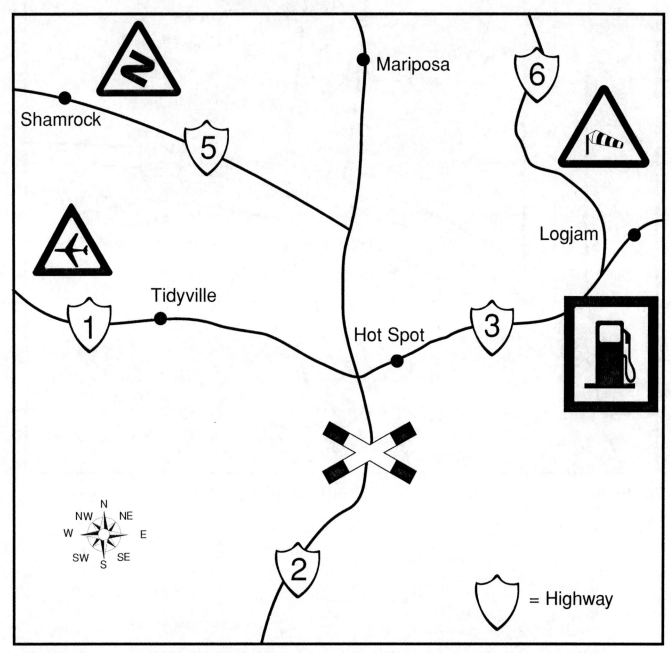

1. Which highway has a nearby gas station? _____

2. What sign is on Highway 1? _____

3. Which highway has winding roads? _____

4. Which highway has a lot of wind? _____

5. Which sign is near Tidyville? _____

6. Which highway crosses railroad tracks? _____

Vacation Spots

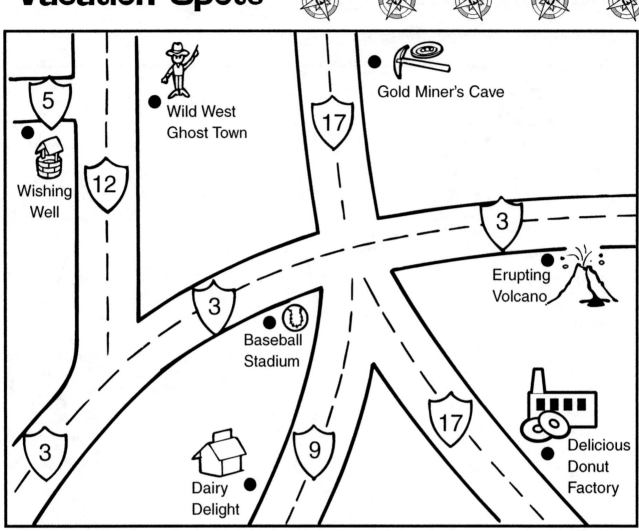

Write the highways used when going from one place to another.

Example: Wishing Well to the Baseball Stadium

Go east on Highway 5, south on Highway 12, and east on Highway 3.

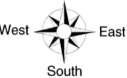

North

West — East

South

1. Gold Miner's Cave to Erupting Volcano _____

_____

2. Dairy Delight to Wild West Ghost Town _____

_____

3. Delicious Donut Factory to the Wishing Well _____

_____

4. Wild West Ghost Town to the Baseball Stadium _____

_____

Hidden Treasure

Draw the path to the hidden treasure by following the directions below. Start at the **X**.

Start

Directions

1. Go up and left over the top of the 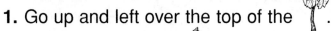 .

2. Go north past the 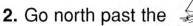 .

3. Go between the 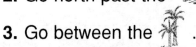 .

4. Stop at the .

5. Go around the north side of the 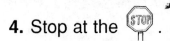 .

6. Go south till you get to the 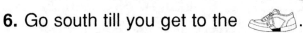 .

7. Go underneath the 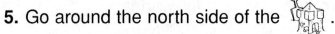 .

8. Go north along the west side of the 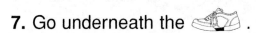 .

9. Go north till you reach the treasure.

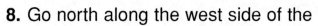
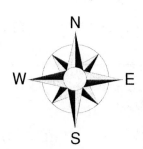

The World

Follow the directions.

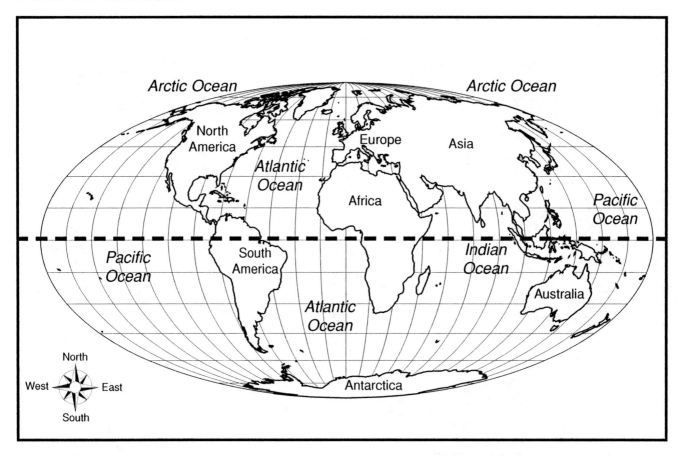

1. The **- - - -** is an imaginary line. It is called the **equator**. The equator divides the world in half. Each half is called a **hemisphere**. Color the equator red.

2. The four continents north of the equator are the following: _____

_____ .

These continents are in the **northern hemisphere**. Color these continents yellow.

3. The three continents south of the equator are the following: _____

_____ .

These continents are in the **southern hemisphere**. Color these continents purple.

4. The oceans on the map are the following: _____

_____ .

Color the oceans blue.

Continents and Oceans

Most of earth is covered in water. These large bodies of water are called **oceans**. There are seven **continents** or land masses and four oceans. Use the map and the clues below to label the oceans and continents.

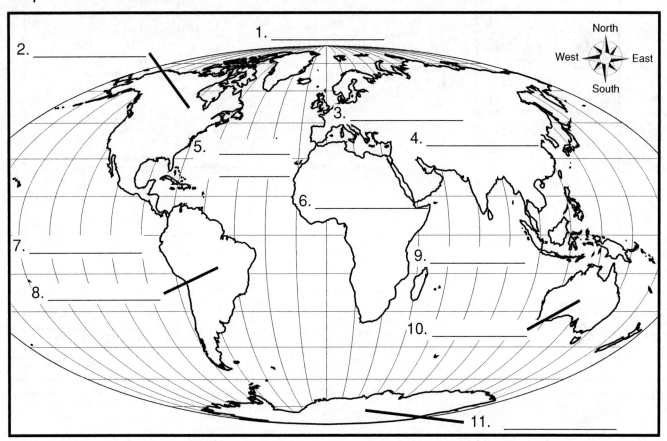

1. _____

2. _____

North
West — East
South

3. _____

4. _____

5. _____

6. _____

7. _____

8. _____

9. _____

10. _____

11. _____

Bodies of Water Clues

- The Arctic Ocean is located on the northernmost part of the map.
- The Pacific Ocean is to the west of North and South America.
- The Atlantic Ocean is between the North American continent and the African continent.
- The Indian Ocean is surrounded by Africa, Asia, and Australia.

Continent Clues

- Antarctica is located on the southernmost part of the map.
- Australia is south of Asia and north of Antarctica.
- South America is south of North America and west of Africa.
- North America is between the Pacific and Atlantic Oceans.
- Africa is south of Europe.
- Europe is to the east of North America and to the west of Asia.
- Asia is east of Europe.

The Emergency Room

Use the map of the emergency room to answer the questions.

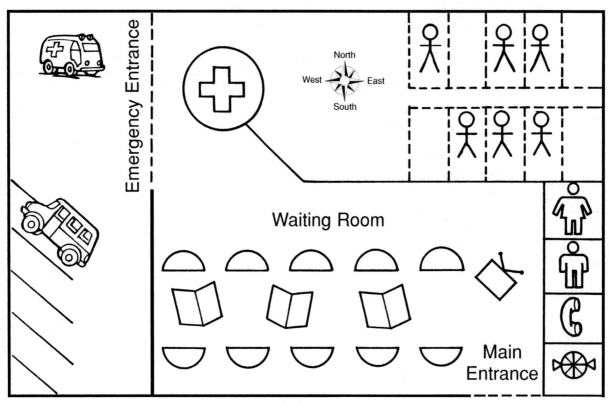

Legend

patient | sliding doors | chair | nurse's station | TV | magazine | emergency room bed | phone | restrooms | snack machine | parking

1. Which side of the building has the emergency entrance to the hospital?

   _____

2. Is the waiting room north or south of the nurse's station?_____

3. On which side of the waiting room are the restrooms located? _____

4. How many people can sit in the waiting room?_____

5. How many beds are in the emergency room?_____

6. How many patients are in the emergency room? _____

7. Is the parking north or south of the ambulance?_____

8. What can people do while sitting in the waiting room? _____

_____

Map Your Classroom

Use the symbols in the legend to draw a map of your classroom.

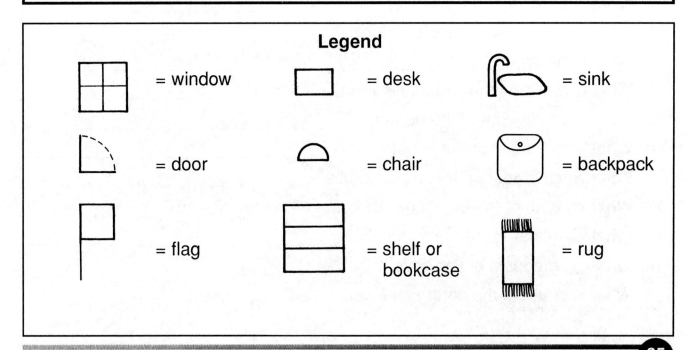

Legend

= window   = desk   = sink

= door   = chair   = backpack

= flag   = shelf or bookcase   = rug

The Pizza Factory

Use the map to answer the questions.

Dough	Pepperoni	Cheese
Veggies	Tomato Sauce	Pineapple

1. What is south of the cheese? _____

2. What is west of the pineapple? _____

3. What is to the east of the veggies? _____

4. What is west of the pepperoni?_____

5. What is to the left of the pineapple? _____

6. What is above the tomato sauce? _____

7. What is below the dough? _____

8. What is between the pineapple and the veggies?_____

9. What is to the right of the dough? _____

10. What is to the left of the tomato sauce? _____

11. What is northwest of the tomato sauce? _____

12. What is north of the pineapple and east of the pepperoni? _____

13. What is southwest of the cheese?_____

14. What is southeast of the dough?_____

15. What is south of the dough and west of the tomato sauce? _____

The Grocery Store

Use the map to answer the questions.

Aisle 1—Fruits	Aisle 5—Desserts
Aisle 2—Vegetables	Aisle 6—Breads
Aisle 3—Drinks	Aisle 7—Bathroom Items
Aisle 4—Meats	Aisle 8—Pet Items

Write the aisle location of the following items.

1. tomatoes _____

2. muffins _____

3. cake _____

4. ham _____

5. milk _____

6. dog shampoo _____

7. toilet paper _____

8. chicken _____

9. toothpaste _____

10. grapes _____

11. orange juice _____

12. wheat bread _____

13. soap _____

14. cookies _____

15. beef _____

16. soda _____

17. bird seed _____

18. toothbrush _____

19. punch _____

20. bananas _____

New Liberty School

Use the map to answer the questions.

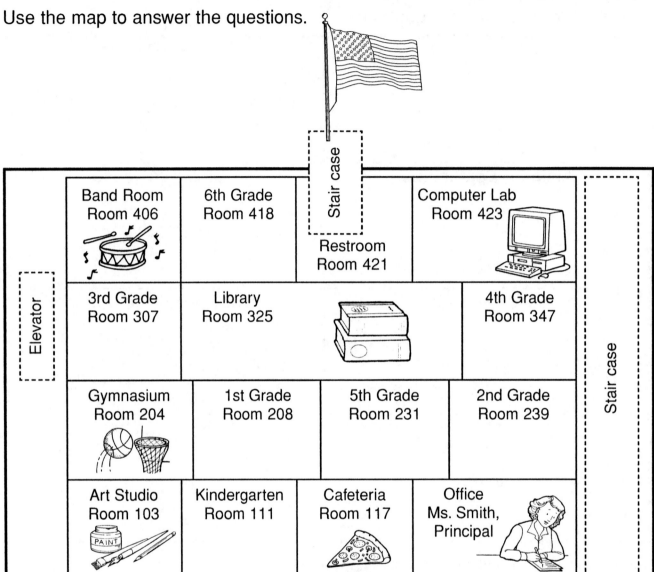

1. On which floor is the principal? _____

2. Is the elevator closer to the Band Room or to the Art Studio? _____

3. Which classrooms are just below the library? _____

4. Which room do you need to use in order to take down the flag? _____

5. On what floor are the restrooms located? _____

6. For what is room 347 used? _____

7. In which room are the 6th graders? _____

8. On which floor is the art studio? _____

My Favorite Place

Make a map showing the layout of your favorite place. Write two questions that can be answered by using the map.

Legend

1. _____

_____

2. _____

_____

Test Practice 1

Fill in the correct answer circle.

1. What is the symbol for "forest"?

 A   B C

2. What is the symbol for "water"?

A B C

3. What is the name of the mountain?

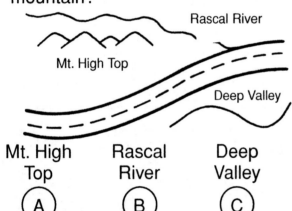

Rascal River

Mt. High Top

Deep Valley

Mt. High Top	Rascal River	Deep Valley
A	B	C

4. How many cabins are there?

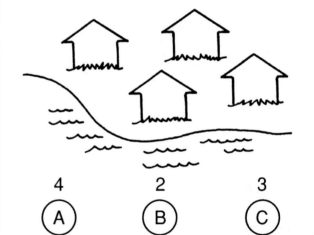

4	2	3
A	B	C

5. Which sign means "driving through a windy area"?

 A   B C

6. Which sign means "cars driving in two directions"?

A   B   C

Test Practice 2

Fill in the correct answer circle.

---

1. How many steps are needed to go from the comb to the key? (*Note*: Each square equals 1 step.)

5	1	3
(A)	(B)	(C)

2. What is northeast of the key?

(A)	(B)	(C)

---

3. What is north of the bubble bath?

(A)	(B)	(C)

4. What is to the left of the duck?

(A)	(B)	(C)

Test Practice 3

Fill in the correct answer circle.

1. What are the directions to go from the Ice Cream Shop to the Pet Shop?

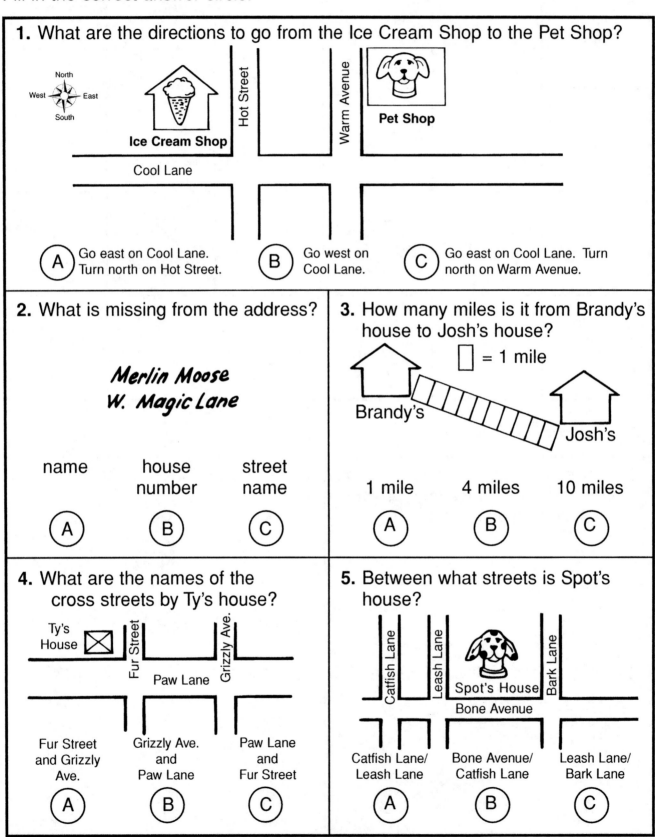

A Go east on Cool Lane. Turn north on Hot Street.

B Go west on Cool Lane.

C Go east on Cool Lane. Turn north on Warm Avenue.

2. What is missing from the address?

Merlin Moose
W. Magic Lane

name — A

house number — B

street name — C

3. How many miles is it from Brandy's house to Josh's house?

☐ = 1 mile

Brandy's   Josh's

1 mile — A

4 miles — B

10 miles — C

4. What are the names of the cross streets by Ty's house?

Ty's House
Fur Street
Paw Lane
Grizzly Ave.

Fur Street and Grizzly Ave. — A

Grizzly Ave. and Paw Lane — B

Paw Lane and Fur Street — C

5. Between what streets is Spot's house?

Catfish Lane
Leash Lane
Spot's House
Bone Avenue
Bark Lane

Catfish Lane/ Leash Lane — A

Bone Avenue/ Catfish Lane — B

Leash Lane/ Bark Lane — C

Test Practice 4

Fill in the correct answer circle.

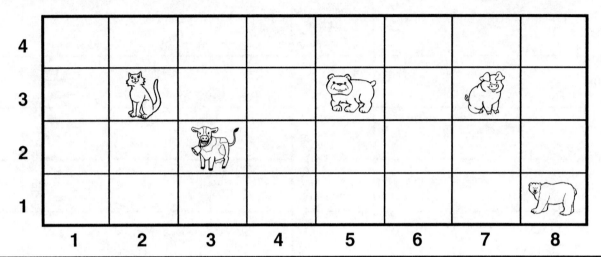

| | 1 | 2 | 3 | 4 | 5 | 6 | 7 | 8 |

1. What is in space (3, 2)?

Ⓐ   Ⓑ   Ⓒ

2. What is right 7 spaces and up 3 spaces?

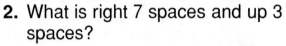

Ⓐ   Ⓑ   Ⓒ

3. What are the coordinate points for the bulldog?

(3, 5)   (5, 3)   (8, 1)

Ⓐ   Ⓑ   Ⓒ

4. What are the coordinate points for the bear?

(3, 5)   (5, 3)   (8, 1)

Ⓐ   Ⓑ   Ⓒ

5. What is north of the star?

Ⓐ   Ⓑ   Ⓒ

6. What is east of the star?

Ⓐ   Ⓑ   Ⓒ

Test Practice 5

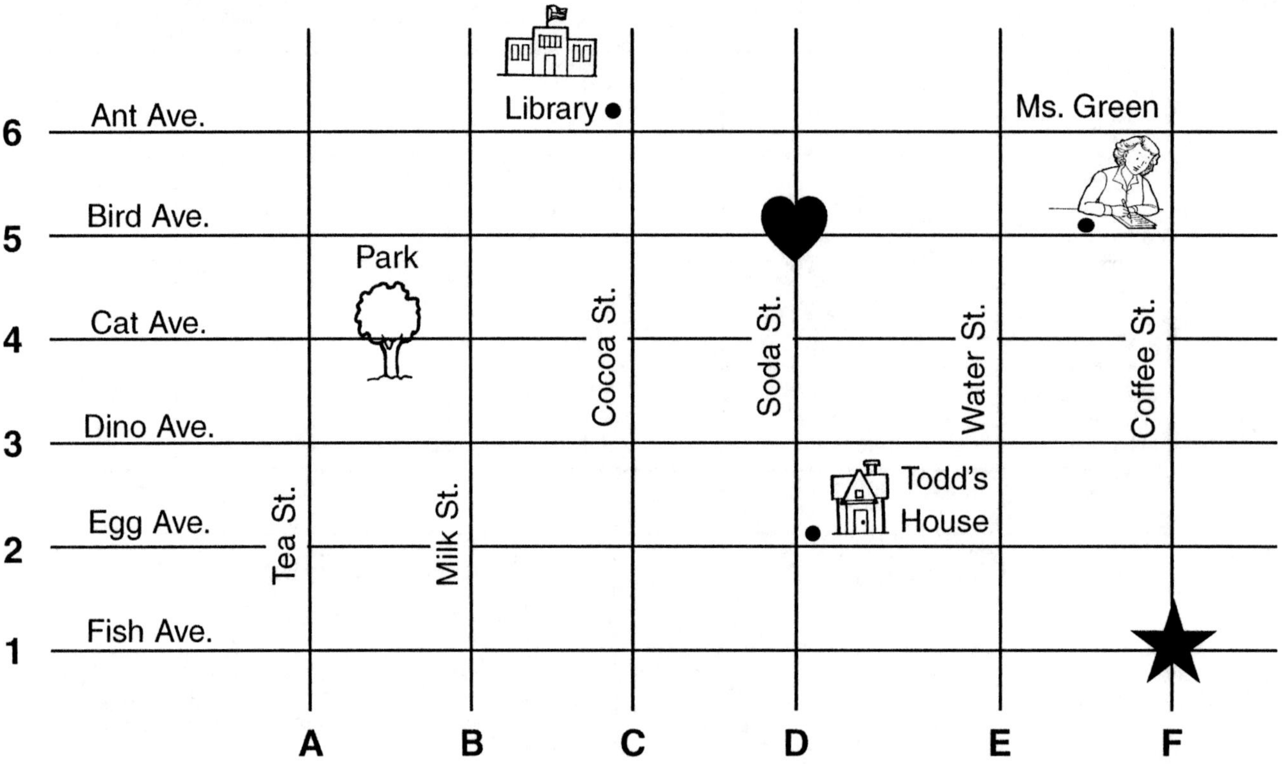

1. On what street does Ms. Green live? Bird Ave. (A) Cat Ave. (B) Dino Ave. (C)	**2.** What is the location of the library? (C, 6) (A) (C, 5) (B) (B, 6) (C)
3. Between what two streets is the park? Cocoa St./ Cat Ave. (A) Bird Ave/ Ant Ave. (B) Tea St./ Milk St. (C)	**4.** What are the cross streets for Todd's house? Coffee St./ Fish Ave. (A) Soda St./ Bird Ave. (B) Soda St./ Egg Ave. (C)
5. Where is the heart located? (F, 1) (A) (D, 5) (B) (D, 4) (C)	**6.** Where is the star located? (D, 5) (A) (F, 1) (B) (F, 2) (C)

Test Practice 6

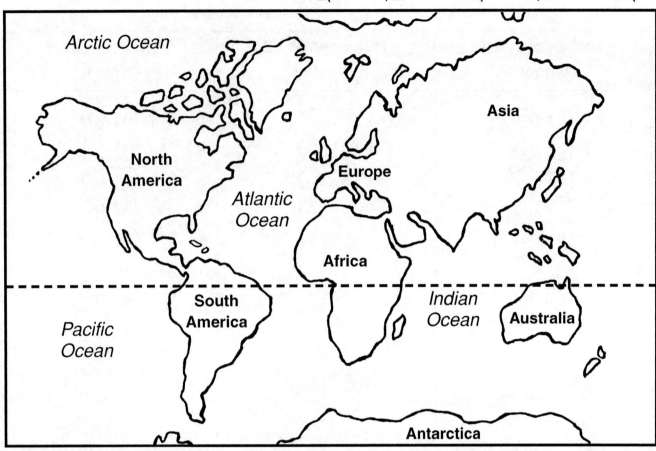

Fill in the correct answer circle.

1. How many continents are there?	2. Which one names an ocean?
5 6 7	Mystery Ocean Pacific Ocean West Ocean
Ⓐ Ⓑ Ⓒ	Ⓐ Ⓑ Ⓒ
3. Which continent is north of South America?	4. What is the name of the ocean off the west coast of Australia?
United States Mexico North America	Pacific Ocean Indian Ocean Arctic Ocean
Ⓐ Ⓑ Ⓒ	Ⓐ Ⓑ Ⓒ
5. Which continent is entirely in the northern hemisphere?	6. Which continent is directly south of Europe?
Asia South America Africa	Australia Asia Africa
Ⓐ Ⓑ Ⓒ	Ⓐ Ⓑ Ⓒ

Answer Sheet

Test Practice 1 Page 40	Test Practice 2 Page 41	Test Practice 3 Page 42
1. Ⓐ Ⓑ Ⓒ 2. Ⓐ Ⓑ Ⓒ 3. Ⓐ Ⓑ Ⓒ 4. Ⓐ Ⓑ Ⓒ 5. Ⓐ Ⓑ Ⓒ 6. Ⓐ Ⓑ Ⓒ	1. Ⓐ Ⓑ Ⓒ 2. Ⓐ Ⓑ Ⓒ 3. Ⓐ Ⓑ Ⓒ 4. Ⓐ Ⓑ Ⓒ	1. Ⓐ Ⓑ Ⓒ 2. Ⓐ Ⓑ Ⓒ 3. Ⓐ Ⓑ Ⓒ 4. Ⓐ Ⓑ Ⓒ 5. Ⓐ Ⓑ Ⓒ
Test Practice 4 **Page 43**	**Test Practice 5** **Page 44**	**Test Practice 6** **Page 45**
1. Ⓐ Ⓑ Ⓒ 2. Ⓐ Ⓑ Ⓒ 3. Ⓐ Ⓑ Ⓒ 4. Ⓐ Ⓑ Ⓒ 5. Ⓐ Ⓑ Ⓒ 6. Ⓐ Ⓑ Ⓒ	1. Ⓐ Ⓑ Ⓒ 2. Ⓐ Ⓑ Ⓒ 3. Ⓐ Ⓑ Ⓒ 4. Ⓐ Ⓑ Ⓒ 5. Ⓐ Ⓑ Ⓒ 6. Ⓐ Ⓑ Ⓒ	1. Ⓐ Ⓑ Ⓒ 2. Ⓐ Ⓑ Ⓒ 3. Ⓐ Ⓑ Ⓒ 4. Ⓐ Ⓑ Ⓒ 5. Ⓐ Ⓑ Ⓒ 6. Ⓐ Ⓑ Ⓒ

Answer Key

Page 4

Drawings may vary.

Page 5

Check to see if symbols are colored correctly.

Page 6

1. 3
2. Emerald Pines
3. Mountain Path
4. Friendly Lodge
5. by car on Road B then Road A
6. by hiking on Mountain Path

Page 7

1. Betsy Ross Mountains
2. Los Amigos
3. western part
4. south
5. south of New Liberty
6. Independence, Happiness, and Justice
7. Highway 7
8. Highway 10
9. east

Page 8

1. You are driving on a winding road.
2. An airport is nearby.
3. Cars are driving in two directions.
4. Children are in the area.
5. Train tracks are up ahead.
6. You are driving through a windy area.
7. Gas station is up ahead.

Page 9

Answers will vary.

Page 10

1. Go south 3 steps. Turn to the west and take 1 step. Or, go west 1 step and south 3 steps.
2. Go north 5 steps turn and go west 4 steps. Or, go west 4 steps and then go north 5 steps.
3. Go east 5 steps. Turn and go south 1 step. Or, go south 1 step and then go east 5 steps.
4. Go south 4 steps. Turn and go west 6 steps. Or, go west 6 steps and then go south 4 steps.
5. Go north 2 steps. Turn and go west 3 steps. Or, go west 3 steps and then go north 2 steps.

Page 11

1. Police Station and Library
2. Bank and Fire Station
3. Police Station and Bank
4. Library and Fire Station
5. east
6. north
7. west
8. south

Page 12

Check to make sure the items were colored correctly.

Page 13

Sample answers: Answers will vary.

1. Bulldog is north of Kitty. Bulldog is west of Turkey.
2. Cow is east of Froggy. Cow is south of Piggy.
3. Piggy is west of Bunny. Piggy is east of Lamb.

4. Kitty is west of Bear. Kitty is south of Bulldog.
5. Turtle is east of cow. Turtle is south of Bunny.

Page 14

1. northwest
2. southeast
3. northeast
4. southwest

Page 15

1. 269 Oak Avenue
2. 540 Maple Street
3. 898 Oak Avenue
4. 535 Elm Street
5. 371 Maple Street
6. 572 Pine Avenue

Page 16

Sample answers: Answers will vary.

1. Go east over the bridge. Then go north.
2. Go north to the picnic area. Turn right and go east over the bridge. Turn left and go north.
3. Go south through the forest to the picnic area. Go east over the bridge until you find the mountains.
4. Go south through the picnic area until you find the cave.
5. Go south. Go west over the bridge. Turn right and go north through the forest till you find the meadow.
6. Go west to the picnic area. Go south till you find the rock.

Page 17

1. 10 miles
2. 15 miles
3. 15 miles
4. 20 miles

Page 18

1. 10 cm or 10 blocks
2. 7 cm or 7 blocks
3. 8 cm or 8 blocks
4. 5 cm or 5 blocks
5. 4 cm or 4 blocks
6. 3 cm or 3 blocks

Page 19

1. Strawberry Lane and Raisin Street
2. Plum Street and Banana Lane
3. Raisin Street and Strawberry Lane
4. Grape Street and Banana Lane

Page 20

1. Blue Street and Red Street
2. Star Avenue and Moon Avenue
3. Red Street and Pink Street
4. Red Street and Pink Street

Page 21

1. 2, 1   4. 5, 4   7. 4, 2
2. 7, 5   5. 4, 6   8. 5, 1
3. 3, 3   6. 6, 2   9. 1, 6

Page 22

1. left 2, down 2
2. left 2, up/down 0
3. right 1, down 1
4. right/left 0, up 2
5. right 4, down 1
6. left 5, up 1
7. right 5, down 1
8. right 1, up 4

Page 23

1. 6, 4   6. 3, 4
2. 7, 6   7. 8, 1
3. 4, 7   8. 3, 8
4. 1, 5   9. 2, 3
5. 5, 2

Answer Key

Page 24

Page 25
1. (A, 6) 6. (H, 2)
2. (C, 1) 7. (C, 4)
3. (F, 5) 8. (G, 3)
4. (F, 1) 9. (A, 3)
5. (E, 2)

Page 26
1. (A, 4) 7. (A, 1)
2. (B, 4) 8. (E, 3)
3. (D, 3) 9. (D, 1)
4. (G, 1) 10. (D, 4)
5. (D, 6) 11. (G, 2)
6. (G, 5) 12. (B, 6)

Page 27
1. school
2. restaurant
3. bowling
4. Girl Scouts
5. bus
6. ambulance
7. Uptown Street
8. Downtown Street
9. Star Avenue
10. Moon Avenue
11. Main Street
12. Sun Avenue

Page 28
1. bus
2. taxi
3. fire engine
4. race car

Page 29
1. 3
2. airport
3. 5
4. 6
5. airport
6. 2

Page 30
1. south on Highway 17, east on Highway 3
2. north on Highway 9, west on Highway 3, north on Highway 12
3. north on Highway 17, west on Highway 3, north on Highway 12, west on Highway 5
4. south on Highway 12, east on Highway 3

Page 31

Page 32
1. equator = red
2. yellow = North America, Africa, Europe, Asia
3. purple = South America, Australia, Antarctica
4. blue = Pacific Ocean, Atlantic Ocean, Indian Ocean, Arctic Ocean

Page 33
1. Arctic Ocean
2. North America
3. Europe
4. Asia
5. Atlantic Ocean
6. Africa
7. Pacific Ocean
8. South America
9. Indian Ocean
10. Australia
11. Antarctica

Page 34
1. west
2. south
3. east
4. 10

5. 10
6. 6
7. south
8. read magazines, watch TV

Page 35
Classroom maps will vary.

Page 36
1. pineapple
2. tomato sauce
3. tomato sauce
4. dough
5. tomato sauce
6. pepperoni
7. veggies
8. tomato sauce
9. pepperoni
10. veggies
11. dough
12. cheese
13. tomato sauce
14. tomato sauce
15. veggies

Page 37
1. Aisle 2
2. Aisle 6
3. Aisle 5
4. Aisle 4
5. Aisle 3
6. Aisle 8
7. Aisle 7
8. Aisle 4
9. Aisle 7
10. Aisle 1
11. Aisle 3
12. Aisle 6
13. Aisle 7
14. Aisle 5
15. Aisle 4
16. Aisle 3
17. Aisle 8
18. Aisle 7
19. Aisle 3
20. Aisle 1

Page 38
1. 1st floor
2. Band Room
3. 1st Grade (Room 208) and 5th Grade (Room 231)
4. Restroom (Room 421)
5. 4th floor
6. 4th Grade
7. Room 418
8. 1st floor

Page 39
Maps will vary.

Page 40
1. B   4. A
2. C   5. C
3. A   6. B

Page 41
1. C
2. B
3. A
4. C

Page 42
1. C
2. B
3. C
4. C
5. C

Page 43
1. A
2. B
3. B
4. C
5. C
6. B

Page 44
1. A
2. A
3. C
4. C
5. B
6. B

Page 45
1. C   4. B
2. B   5. A
3. C   6. C